WEAVING NESTS WITH SMOKE AND STONE

ISBN 978-1-877010-71-2

Walleah Press
PO Box 368
North Hobart
Tasmania 7002
Australia
Email: admin@walleahpress.com.au

Cover design/photography: Lynda Warner

Walleah Press

WEAVING NESTS WITH SMOKE AND STONE

Gina Mercer

For Eric & Gillian
to enjoy the nest of
birds & words —
Gina M

CONTENTS

Blue dusk pours down

flick   flirt   flicker

solo grey fantail
sweet active flycatcher
acrobats above the pool

fast, last-minute dancer
flickering the falling stillness

fossicking in chill air
for invisible insect snacks
to fill her miniscule belly
before the no-fly night prevails

flick   flirt   flicker

her deft arabesques inscribe
a casual, perfect script
across the amphitheatre of air

agile feathered bones
defy
all physics
all falling

Where the gale goes

It's tough weather for flying,
wings won't hold position
as winter coruscates the island.

A musk lorikeet attempts
to fly from one wind-wrought
                                        eucalypt to another.

She does an Emily Dickinson:
flying true
but flying slant.
She arrives, cautioning others –
stay in your hollows,
this wind is no friend to feathers.

Even the commuter stream
of silver gulls is absent
from this dangerous sky.

One lone Pacific gull,
on high, rides the gale,
abandoning all notion of destination,
going where the gale drives –

          out to sea.

* "Tell all the truth but tell it slant". Emily Dickinson, Poem 1263.

Larus pacificus

Winter storms toss onto the tideline
a Pacific gull, *Larus pacificus.*

Once-solid head now lolls and flops
at each fresh push of wave.

Large yellow feet clench and curl
like a preschooler's nervous fingers.

Alive, these gulls impress,
stance confident, bulk imposing,
stolid shoulders, peremptory stare,
outclassing the needy silver gulls.

Look closely at the glazed tangle –
the massive saffron beak
is tipped, tenderly, with lipstick pink,
          Larus pacificus.

Vivid

The arriving chatter of musk lorikeets
interrupts our toast communion.

Abandoning coffee cups,
hands fossick for binoculars.

Three birds are feeding on blossom
in that young gum we planted.

Peering through misted lenses
we discern compact bright-green bodies
angling around luscious filaments,
red-tipped beaks dipping deep in creamy skirts.

Theirs is the palette of the tropics:
red, green, yellow – strong,
sharp shapes contrasting
the muted messy glory of the gum.
It too is clad in red and green,
shiny ochre stems accenting sage-green leaves.

Chatting to one another like lorikeets
passing the binoculars back and forth,
we finish breakfast and pack for work.

Bustling into one more beige-busy day
we cradle the small, bird miracle
that landed, vivid, in our garden
as we sat eating toast.

The office worker makes a bird list

A small flock of brush wattlebirds charging intently across the yard;
a solo silvereye (*unusual that, they generally travel in pods*);
a gaggle of goldfinch gathering for an early morning sip at the pond;
a female blackbird (*largely brown, in spite of her name*);
a New Holland honeyeater perusing the world from the topmost
                    tip of a melaleuca;
a pair of corellas landing all raggedy in that big old blue-gum;
a pair of green rosellas looping the park (*clearly it's a morning for*
                    paired parrots);
a funereal stand of lesser pied cormorants hanging their wings
                    out to dry;
a lone Pacific gull, bouncer gauging the crowd;
one silver gull breakfasting by dibbling scarlet feet in liquid sand,
                    lifting
        small gastropods from their secret roads;
a family of welcome swallows, swinging in the air,
        low down, beside the water,
        resting on the flat black rocks, chatting,
        an outing with recently fledged young (*I think*);
and that gang of immaculate sulphur-crested cockatoos,
        raucousing around, making sure the world is aroused…

all this   already
before the day at the desk begins.

Italy is empty

Jenny's ailing,
the cancer's called again –
determined to take her
        for one final waltz.

Jenny's longing
for the quickstep of travel,
for the Italy she's never seen.
She rings the bank and her best friend,
cancels treatments,
books a date of a different kind.

Jenny's flying,
prosecco and tiramisu all the way,
no need to worry
about her liver, her weight,
        longevity.

Jenny's returning,
friends cluster eager.
Jenny says –
Yes, yes, marvellous time,
but I really missed the birds.
Apart from the pigeons in Rome,
there were no birds.
Italy felt, it felt kind of empty. No birds.

Jenny's sliding,
lying in her own bed,
finding solace in the abundance
of her own backyard –
this bird-music all she wants
          to accompany
her final waltz.

Messenger?

Silent masked owl
flies in one window
        circles
study
lounge
kitchen
bedroom –

on hissing wings
she circles thrice
our bright-lit rooms –

two weeks after your death.

After the gales

We are two ancient fence posts
leaning together
in the blighted corner of the paddock.

Only just
          standing.

Leaning into and onto,
   just
      holding up.

Lichen grows over
the weather of our timber,
reaches a tentative finger
across the touching edges,

joining us – fragile –
against the gales.

Holding on
Jamieson Valley, Blue Mountains

Two women in pastel, crimplene skirt-suits,
neglected-cupboard hats and orthopaedic shoes

hasten along the wheelchair-wide, clifftop path
holding hands,
          holding on to human.

This wide rushing air,
this canyon of blue and green,
this endless echoing space

terrifies

after so many decades
within cream ward walls.

The spider of affection

As you rinse spuds
the delicate spider of affection
tickles lightly down your back.

Tonight she'll tiptoe a halo
of the lightest thread
round your sleeping head,
weave a canopy of silken knots.

She'll wake you by dancing
eight petite feet on your cheek
in time for you to bathe
in the intricacies of sunrise.

Off the window-ledge of the everyday
she drops suddenly
          on delicate thread
                    to acrobat across your view.

Small essential spider
spinning us whole each day.

What the marigolds do

In a hungry rush,
you unpackage their lanterns,
rip through the dingy recycled paper,
plunge their stolid, furry stems
into hopeful water.

All evening the marigolds lumber in the vase,
faces sullen, reading the wood grain of the table,
performing the shapes of wet rope.

You emerge next morning,
to discover
they have drunk their fill,
faces lifting,
throwing whoops of orange
up to the white ceiling.

As you mull over your muesli,
they sing *a cappella* with the daffodils,
elegant riffs of saffron sound.

Why all the embarrassment about being happy
when a bunch of marigolds can get there
simply by drinking a nightful of water?

* The italicised line is from Wendell Berry's poem, 'Why'.

Working at simplicity

My mind is a paddock, full of grass and sky.

The grey mice of anxiety scuttle in,
plaguing and creeping
tussock to tussock.

The hawks of doubt wheel,
dark, angular cut-outs, threatening
the simplicity of blue.

The wallabies of practicality
arc across the open,
sparking with ideas:
what to, how to, when to....

How hard it is, to make my mind –

a paddock
full of nothing
but grass and sky.

Portrait of eastern rosellas with small girl

She must be five years old,
though she looks smaller
in her grey-blue, size-too-big blazer
plaits afuzz in the afternoon air.

She treads the grass softly, following
a pair of rosellas
as they waddle low and plump
about the playground
ignoring shouts, boys, sticks,
brimming strollers and errant balls.

Two solemn birds in lairy plumage
oblivious to the bustle of dangers –

or perhaps they sense
the potent protection
of a small girl's veneration?

Portrait of white cockatoos and walnut tree

A racket of cockatoos
flaps and rasps the soft grey air.

The birds' destination,
an old walnut tree, serene and rounded
as an eighteenth century painting.

The white cockatoos alight,
sulphur crests angled precisely,
poised as white-robed choristers.
Elegant shapes contrast
the tree's rich, summer green.

For once they are silent, intent,
each clasps a globe in one steady claw,
beaks busy, peeling
the green and white layers of walnuts.

Quiet walkers turn their ears,
a new sound intrigues:
the clear yet gentle ticking
of cockatoo beaks on crisp nut flesh.

Small change

A small suburban block. Nothing startling. Garden motley. The only residents, a bodgie gang of blackbirds who dominate the real estate. Forests of weeds flourish. We set to. Weed and dig and mulch and terrace. Spurn the dwarf conifers and lavender hedges the suburb favours. Bed only local plants into the freshly turned earth. Dig a pond. Frogs arrive, mysterious. What songline tells them of new water? How do they navigate arid bitumen? They make themselves at home, call so vigorously the neighbours can't hear their TVs. Rosellas, green and eastern, begin to drop in for a drink. All winter, honeyeaters feed here on the island's subtle blossom. Kunzia perfume teaches us to breathe in new ways. Rampant bushiness asserts itself. Neighbours finger electric hedge trimmers. Bird calls renovate our days. Frog songs lullaby our nights.

Variable goshawk

The grey goshawk isn't –
not a single fleck of colour
graces this gliding vase.

Every feather is pure white
like the frost-wrapped rocks at Dove Lake.

The *only all-white raptor in the world*
is roosting in my neighbour's elm
scanning the earth for skinks.

The walled green world goes hush,
inhabitants awed (or terrified) by this presence.
Immaculate, this morph seems mythic.

It is pure stillness
except for those garnet-red eyes
swivelling slow as interstellar radar
scanning the small horizon
for inattentive flesh.

Soaring is, perhaps, not effortless.
The goshawk rests an hour
among comforting leaves
then lifts smooth   up
into the valley's spiralling air.

Angling the winter-white sky
it flies beyond opacity
exquisitely camouflaged
to ambush wrens and starlings
as they bustle about
their tiny, shrub-bound lives.

* Australia's grey goshawk has a white variant or morph, most common in Tasmania.

* Quotes (in italics) are from *Birds in Backyards* and *Parks and Wildlife (Tasmania)* websites.

Spoonbill and swan

a circle of prosperous trees
a paper-white circle of sand
a lake of amber tea

sister and daughter
stroll across the lake
tossing a grass-nest of concerns

tears trickle on daughter's ripe apricot face

sister reaches to embrace
her paper-white shoulders

as they touch
daughter becomes a spoonbill
sister a crisp-edged black swan

wings tangle
white on black and white

their wing-clumsy embrace persists
until they are close and calm
as the trees the sand the lake

Audrey and Charles dance

Mt Wellington gathers a grey flock of dusk to its shoulders.

Brushing elbows and lips,
after a day of mutual solitude,
they meet in their shabby living-room,
touch hands,
pour each other a drink:
Scotch (no ice) for her,
driest red for him.

They sip   and toast each other.

The golden ash outside their window
pours autumn light up to the ceiling.

This pair is not autumnal,
they are spare winter,
savaged and pared.

Music bathes the light-rich room.
They begin to dance, their nightfall ritual.

She caretakes his knees,
he is mindful of her hip
as they swivel and dip.

Bone-clear,
          they dance,
two ancient blue-gums.

She walks, and walks

It's Tasmania, where every day might
give rain, or extreme sun,
or windstorm, or soft mizzle.

There's Little Red Riding Hood,
the tiny woman who,
whatever the weather, walks, and walks.

She's wearing her trademark rainjacket,
the one that comes down past her knees.
All we see is the moving jacket
tilting forward into the weather
propelled by the skinniest of shins
and small, black-shod-sensible feet.

It's relentlessly wet today.
Driving by in my warm-lush car
I see Red Riding Hood out walking,
walking through the unarguable rain.

It looks, impossibly, like her shins have shrunk.
I have a sudden image of her arriving home,
shrugging off her hood,
stripping down to slightly
saggy knickers and childsize singlet.

I imagine a generous, warm, fluffy towel
to dry the stretched strings of flesh
that so barely clothe her spindle-bones.

Her feet, unshod for once,
resilient as elderly sparrows.
I want to clasp each one in tender hands,
massage their frail ferocity,
gift them just a few rare minutes of rest,
before she sets off
          to walk, and walk,
                    whatever the weather.

Mother-daughter rain

Monsoon pummels the garden
we rain-dance beneath the wet, wet trees –
eyes showering laughter.

Open the window

all the birds in my brain
fly out

some
zoom and pirouette
across the garden's stage
confident of audience

some
glide smooth,
land on sturdy branches,
roost to converse

some
hop flitter
consider the window
take their own watchful time

all the birds in my brain
fly out

The effects of immersion

Immersing myself in birds,
gradually, I find,
my hair   begins
to flick out in   odd   places
                feathers in a strong wind.

Strangest of all, right
        where a woman's wings might sprout,
that touchable spot
just below the shoulder blades, right
there, a peculiar ache grows,

as if something is burgeoning,
        something wants to get out.

Resilience

Nasturtiums are growing in my pelvis

curling a bright way
        around the arc of hip sockets,

coiling fearless tendrils
        through furled anatomy,

dancing piquant umbrella leaves
        above all the sweet spaces –

unfurling riots of gladness,
        singing clear vermilion.

Waking up poem

Forget

all you know about Canute,
the king who believed the waves under his dominion,
he could stop the tides by command.

Remember

to bet all you have
          on the dead cert

that global warming is real

                    as real as the Incas are extinct.

Oh, to be a swamp snake now the rains are here

Every spangled surface teems,
water busy in nippled skeins.
Grass springs angles, clumped and tousled
by pip-slippery frogs' arousal.
Succinct and lilliputian leaps,
delicate-neat as sushi heaps,
plump, bejewelled, handmade sweets,
frogs slick-dancing to monsoon beats.

Oh, to be a swamp snake now,
lying luxurious – all anyhow.
The grace and lap of slowly feeding,
no haste, no chase, no ache-needing,
fig-opulent, skin stretched pregnant,
full-length, lustrous, joy-tight serpent.

Still dancing

Simple suburban street effervesces –
plum blossom everywhere

except on this one old tree.
The warm caress of spring
has failed to arouse
this craggy tree whose perfume
was so opulent, unexpected.

Look sadly at its black, bloomless twigs
then observe, on the smooth cream paling fence

the tree is performing
          in crisp silhouette
                    an exquisite tracery
of moving shadows –

          old tree still dancing.

The language of physics

rises up
as she walks, absorbing
the valley's teeming,
walking inside the physics.

Gravity draws the fine rain
down to the rich valley floor,
evaporation activates droplets
to atomise, stir,
                    to glisten
inexorably up.

The air is teeming with wet,
she can almost see the view
populated by those red and blue arrows
beloved of physics teachers.

A rosella,
coloured royally crimson and blue,
performing the laws of aerodynamics and propulsion,
          swoops,
itself a vivid arrow,
                    across the fervent grey air –

You are gentle, even with the fish

You decide to study fish,
how they live and breed
in tiny coral caves
on a remote reef
perched out in the Pacific.

You dive and dive,
discover they maneuvre
their eggs' hatching
to match the full moon.
Tiny glimmers of possibility
adrift in the ocean's shimmer.

The fish you choose
are not flashy, they're small,
animated gold disks
gleaming above
blue-lilac coral forests.

You need to find a way
to identify each one,
to see if they roam the reef nomadic
or dwell for years in a favoured coral cave.

You ponder and toss, how
to mark each fish.
Most use tags,
shooting staples into filmy flesh.

This seems too vicious.
You ponder and read,
diving into published studies,
seeking a subtler way.

You grow an idea:
you'll approach a cave,
bathe each fish in sleeping potion
then, as they slumber and rock,
beneath the dorsal fin
you'll place a tiny dot tattoo,
unique, discreet.

You need ink,
but burly tattooists
aren't buying your story.
You earnestly explain,
biologist's beard aquiver:
you only want to tattoo fish.

They laugh grimly,
seeing you as competition,
or worse, a nutter,
muscle you out the door.

Finally you find a bloke
who's intrigued, he's tattooed
pigs but never fish, he says.
He sells you all the ink you need,
makes you promise to come back
to tell him how it goes.

You help the fish to sleep,
inscribe them, weigh them
in a special cradle you've designed
to weigh creatures underwater,
(no mean feat),
and wait.

You light up when you find
your tattooed golden damsels
swim on unperturbed,
feeding blithely on
algal salads and shrimp cocktails.

They survive for years,
residing in their coral caves,
breeding with lunatic precision
every full flood moon.

Once, in turmoil
I had to choose between you and another.
I thought of you and your slumbering, golden *damoiselles* –

I chose you
because you are gentle,
even with the fish.

Seahorse farm

Newborns waver in clear water
thin and black, needy as leeches.

Six-month-olds tangle and glide
in hydropet tubs of salty river.
One prehensile tail curls,
strangles another,
in slow-motion
the strangled untangles,
drifts away from danger,
away from that feckless furl of fish flesh,
gratefully grasping
the plastic mesh on which they roost –
moving rococo scrollwork.

Adults dance in their glass-sided vat,
graceful as mating butterflies.
Two seahorses intent upon each other,
they pair for life,
his pearly potbelly drift-dancing,
flicker-tickled by her shimmering fin.

They'll dance again for human delight,
aquarium captives destined
to be the final decorative touch
in some highrise aluminium apartment.

All their lives in glass cases –
never free to dance
in the swell and belly of the sea.

Sleek otter of sleep

Sea-silver otter of sleep
swims to your side,
wreathing lithe
around your sad shoulders.

Gently she chirrups,
calling down the sweet swoon,
your muscles slide,
soothed, to her rhythms of rest.

She hums a soft air into
the curl of your neck,
feathers your cheek
with nimble whiskers,
enfolds you
in fronds of kelp,
pillows you
on the billowing swell.

Sleek otter of sleep
sings you, swims you
        into the darkling-deep
                ocean of dream.

Knowing bitter air

Melbourne

See these paperbarks
leaning languid
against the bluestone wall,
edging the wrought-iron street,
loose hair tangling
in straight-laced guttering,
creamy trunks
girdled by metal teeth.

They cannot fathom
the fashions of industry,
why they breathe this bitter air,
so unlike the glittering, scented draughts
their ancestors swallowed free.

See these tree-ferns
proffering delicate solace
beneath the paperbarks,
roots curling in distaste
at the chemical underground,
gracious parasol curves
longing for the shelter of deep-valley forests,
lamenting the pervasive
spackle of this rushing street.

See the make-busy animals who live here
hectic with electronic mating and high-speed slumber.

Who will be kind to the make-busy animals
who live here, so far from the languid days,
who sense the change in times,
who breathe the bitter air,

and know they made it so?

Outlook

A chatty family of goldfinch
trampolining on grassheads,
feeding on the flourishing lawn.

Time to mow, he says.

The animals call

Plot to plot
the animals call.
Angle grinders and buzz saws
scrawling their howls, white-hot
across the aching afternoon.

The animals meander down
to the electric blue waterhole
in the gritty dusk,
wallow their cushiony bodies
in the grid-neat chemical cool.

In the dark brown itch of evening
the animals set their TVs
to murmur secrets
each to each
across fenceless corridors of air
between their brick square lairs.

Walk beyond

We walk beyond
the muddling families
hurling snowballs and commands,
dropping beanies and gloves,
slip-sliding on trampled, muddied ice
in their pink Barbie gumboots,
slumping uggboots, and
pale suede heels.

We walk beyond
the council barriers
into the snow-scape.
The higher we climb,
the sparser the people-scape,
until there is only
the percussion of our boots
squtching in icy puddles,
crisp-crunching on clear ice,
whispering through fresh drifts,
sloshing in free-running melt.

We walk beyond, up
beneath the Organ Pipes,
vertical pillars of warm-brown rock
capped with neat snow berets.

Walk beyond
a sense of sore knees and self,
onto the mountain's flank
into the rhythm of
          tree and snow,
          rock and air,
into the mountain's breathing –

Transubstantiation

Rain decorates, soaks, my shirt,
rain-fingers rearrange my hair
firm as any high priestess hairdresser.

The bus-tour-busy lookout is deserted,
only rain drops populate the concrete apron.
They're all singularly unimpressed with the vista.
Seen it all before.

Released from the comfort of cloud
each drop takes its task seriously,
getting straight down to the work
dictated by that eternal task-master, gravity,
who forbids all distractions or deviations,
prohibits meandering from the prescribed path.
Even following such strictures,
the raindrops enjoy
stunning visions all the way down.

Reaching their earthly destination
they slow,   dissipate,
revel in green and private views
inside the lucent gills of plants
until transpiration releases them
to the leisurely sights of evaporation.

They are freed, floating, transubstantiating
up to join fresh cloud congregations.

No wonder they're unimpressed
with this magnificent vista,
they've seen it all before,

aeons and aeons of views
residing inside each ancient drop.

Soundscapes

Blue Mountains

I: Sliding Light

The constant whoosh of waterfalls and tour buses
punctuated by the gargling semicolons of wattlebirds,
the exclamation marks of white cockatoos.

II: Zinging Air

Hoosh of wind pushing a cold front,
carolling of currawongs,
kids calling, effervescing from the corral of school.

III: Taste of Citrus

Shirr of a cyclist's tyre rounding
a corner on frosted bitumen.

Satin bowerbird mimicking
the cries of a lost kitten.

That rhododendron singing
the hallelujah chorus in high cerise.

About this morning's phone call…

Yesterday
        you showed me
                the magnificence of rhododendrons,
                        the significance of green-hoods.

Today
        I showed you
                insensitivity –

blundering a question about your dead child
into that soft, early-morning heart.

Your tears run all the way down to my blunt elbow.

Vanquishing grey

Three jonquils in a glass
breathe shafts of sun
into the winter bathroom.

Ode to the sublime plurality of small brown birds

I glimpse a small, determined shape
through a curtain of casuarina,
a curving tail of such symmetry a sculptor's fingers twitch,
a body so compact a car designer sighs.

I stop tramping,
watch through a crosshatch of twigs,
imagine the exquisite apparatus of your kidneys,
the filigree capillaries of your fine-wire legs.

I travel over shale and gravel,
your songs counterpointing
my light, crunching rhythms.
You trill and reel and ripple and tick.
Your syncopation awakens the tussocky hills.

Dull and drab, some call you,
brown and boring.

Your colour palette is delicate,
eye-resting hues of grey edging to brown,
dottles of olive and brushes of russet,
on a steady ground of brown edging to grey.

The bird book may name you
jenny wren, scrub tit, thornbill, whistler,
grassbird, field wren, silvereye, pipit and *thrush.*
May berate you for being difficult
to differentiate from other 'Little Brown Jobs',
or LBJs, as the twitchers casually dismiss you.

Blunt senses miss your magnificence,
but I sing your birdness.

You enliven eyes, energise ears,
arouse our city-silted hearts
with your extravagantly
ordinary
life.

Being voted Australia's favourite bird

makes not a jot of difference
to your capacity to carol and dive.

Three of you stand on the lawn looking hungry,
fat as the illustrious Italian tenors
and just as handsomely attired,
though juvenile's suit is somewhat dusky,
as if he's frolicked in a puddle of dust
on the way home from some post-performance party.

Your music is equally famous,
adored accompaniment to our mornings,
your arias relished for purity and complexity.

No one admires your ferocity,
your Spring offensive, your diving attacks
on naive strollers and cyclists.
You're not deflected by foils or reflectors,
shrill whistles or desperate arms.
Your beak's aim, accurate as your song,

precision, your signature.

Tell us ’bout Old Joe, the galah

Well, old Joe, ’e was quite the meanest bird I ever knew. We saved ’im from a nest. The bloody ants ’ad eaten all the other nestlings. ’Orrible sight. Anyway, I know you science types don’t go much on birds ’aving their own personalities but old Joe, ’e was a mean bastard from the get-go. And bloody clever. Pretty quick smart, ’e learned to whistle the dog, sounded exactly like Dad’s whistle. And I mean, identical, bloody impeccable. So, the bird would whistle the dog, the mutt’d come lolloping over to the cage, all slobber and tongue and dumb enthusiasm. Joe’d hold out his biscuit through the wire, offer it to the fool animal. Well, what hungry farm dog can say no to a biscuit at the end of the day?

Soon as the dog’s face got close, eyes fixed on that biscuit, Joe’d go for it. ’E’d peck the bejesus out of the dog’s nose, mouth, eyes, any part of the poor bloody mutt ’e could reach. Talk about vicious. The dog’d be yelpin’, trying to pull away but old Joe, no way was ’e gunna let go. And you know how strong a parrot’s beak is? Well, let’s just say, them beaks, they’re designed to crack tough nuts. You can imagine what one of those bastards can do when applied, vicious-like, to a dog’s mouth. I tell you, it was on for young and old. The dog’d be yelping, Joe’d be hangin’ on, and Dad’d come runnin’ full pelt across the yard yellin’ blue murder, all us kids followin’. Complete bloody circus. Finally we’d drag the miserable mutt away, take ’im in for mum to patch up a bit.

Then Dad'd 'ave a good yell at Joe, curse 'im from 'ere to Sunday. And Joe? Well, 'e'd bung it on, lookin' all downhearted, hunchin' himself up in the corner as if 'e were the one hardly done by. Then 'e'd call out, *Joe wants a biscuit.* Course, Dad always said *No bloody way* to that, after all this malarkey. What do you reckon Joe'd do then? Well, 'e'd empty 'is water tin, stick 'is head inside, and cough. Why? Why do you reckon? Yep, you guessed it, the empty tin amplified the sound. Ever heard a galah coughing inside a tin? I can tell you, it sounds bloody dire, as if the bird's at death's door. I don't know how 'e knew about amplification but as sure as my name is Bluey, that bird knew exactly what 'e was doing. Worked every time. One of us kids would feel right sorry for the bastard bird. We'd wait til Dad was off on the tractor, sneak by and drop a biscuit in Joe's cage, fill his tin. It was 'ot out there, couldn't leave 'im without water, could we? Then the stage'd be set for the whole bloody show to go again. Yeah, old Joe, he was one mean bastard of a bird, right from the get-go. But smart, bloody smart, you gotta give 'im that.

The lapwings move upmarket

The neighbours raise a roof,
build themselves a whole new floor.

A sing of lapwings
eschews the traditional
scrape on the ground nest,
with *sparse lining of twigs, stones*
and animal droppings.

They move up in the world,
nest amid the rectangular ridges
of this brand-new aluminium roof,
best view in the street.

No fear here of
boys wielding curious sticks,
careless joggers' feet,
the hunting mouths of dogs.

Builders' noise is replaced
by lapwing alarm cries
as they patrol and defend
their untrammelled, avant-garde territory.

Such ingenuity, such daring,
but will their *four blotched olive eggs*
survive this shiny brave new world?

* Quotes (in italics) are from Slaters' *Field Guide to Australian Birds,* 2008, p 98.

Fuelled by courage

They have russet rumps,
the silvereyes of Tasmania.
They're plumper, more dapper,
than their mainland cousins.

Share the same bad habits,
pillaging fruit, from figs to peaches,
descending on vineyards, scheming
their way under elaborations of netting.

Every autumn, these minuscule birds,
fuelled by courage and ancient logic,
fly from Tasmania to Noosa.

Eleven grams and eleven centimetres of bird,
they gather in cogent flocks,
traverse two thousand kilometres of air and storm.

No one's sure why.
And these days, some are reconsidering,
abandoning the tradition of migration.
Imagine the complex deliberations.

Is greater courage needed
to endure months
of frost-lined nests and shrinking bellies,
or to fly predatory skies,
alpine, ocean, city –
        flying perilous,
                flying so far beyond?

Crested hawk

Above the nest's edge
beaks of baby birds
poke upwards
convenient
as handles on a shopping basket.

A crested hawk
all sleek steel-blue power
plumbs the tree,
accurate
as German engineering.

A currawong is a swoop,

calls skywrite loops across the echoing sky,

        wings carve swoops between the gum trees,

yellow eyes scoop sun-sleepy lizards sideways.

Tristania

Climbing,
my sapling limbs
know the way, up
into the canopy,
into the mother-depths
                    of this old *Tristania.*

Bark crunch-peels to dusky pink,
deeply cool and smooth,
the colour of beloved flesh.
Shapely leaves swish secrets to one another,
creamy flowers burst their innocence
into the redolent sky.

On a branch as wide as my waist,
I stretch out on my back,
absorb the choreography
of limbs, leaves, clouds, birds.

Or loll on my stomach,
cheek pressed against silken bark,
dancing wild green words in my head.

Cool velvet underfoot

Monday morning, the park is active.
Lean executives jog relentless,
cyclists commute, flashing diligence,
middle-agers circumnavigate in comfort-plump shoes.

Arid and tired,
I step feckless,
my feet tasting
the cool velvet of grass.

Too exhausted to muster a goal,
my hungry arms angle round my ribs.

Ambling aimless – I am the park's only epicure.

Even the sky is in peak-hour frenzy:
six ibis speed an invisible path
like girls cycling late to school,
an arrow of magpie geese creaks off to work.

Only that kestrel looks weary as it flap flap glides
home from hunting the night.

Apart from me and a worm-supping, dew-sipping peewee,
no one enters the park's centre.
All so purposeful, oblivious,
so busy, skirting,

this simple,
grass-gorgeous park.

The geometry of change

Heat lounges,
a slumbering cinnamon tabby,
fur sticking to all the city's crevices.

Pedestrian faces flush cerise
as we toil the glaring pavements.

Cool change sweeps up the river.

The cinnamon tabby arches slowly,
          stalks off.

Wild and angled
          hair lifts
from heat-bloated heads.

Birds and leaves zoom
          random trajectories
across the crazy air.

The town shrugs, brushes itself off,
                    revels in the anarchy of wind.

Walking the Ross River after work

My mind is a ball-bearing factory
aclatter with jitter and clutter.

I must walk.

Sun lights on my armskin
like a mother's gentle rousing.

On the egg-blue edge of sky
swallows embroider baroque scrolls.

Flounces of callistemon blossom
perfume the air ecstatic.

Lorikeet gossip ripples my ear –
natter about the nectar.

Wild ducks, so neat and complete,
ride the silken grace of water.

Jacanas dance light
across the lily-pads, rare
kinetic bouquets.

Elegant in russet, black and white,
a brahmini kite scans the river for dinner.

The heron is white, pure origami,
utterly still at the steely water's edge.

My legs stride calm,
air easing on muscle like oil on steel.

Ancient restorative

Stand on the beach
wrap the sky around you.

Lie on the sand
open everything to the sun.

Wade into the ocean
wash away bitter tension.

Walk the sea wind
release all bonds.

Gaze at the diving gannets –
become one.

Amplitude

South-west Western Australia

Awed by the eloquence of trees
we pause in this karri forest.
The only sound
a calligraphy of small
                                        falling
                                                leaves.

Child backseat sulking
wants a drive-through forest
accompanied by Hit Machine Volume 4.
We prefer the drifting silence.

Rounding the next corner
a blaring
        amplitude of ocean.
The vigour of its colour
making the postcards look pale.

Embedded

Your memory's struggling, that's why the computer's slow.
Clean out the embedded images, that'll free up some megabytes.

I investigate, find hundreds (yes, actually hundreds)
of pictures of cute animals I've never seen.
Cute animals. Really?

There's a kitten in a Santa hat (of course),
a tiny grey squirrel curled, shivering, under a coating of snow,
a baby hippo bathing in a blue plastic tub,
a sequence of guilt-ridden dogs, Puritan placards
round their necks proclaiming their 'crimes':
I ate the house-sitter's false teeth.

There's a corpulent possum eating a tray of fruit tarts,
forty biggish bears slumping in every fork of a puny pine tree,
a baby porcupine sleeping on its back
(not so cute, this one, more shiny-pink naked repellent),
two pandas apparently committing a break-and-enter
(inevitable folksy caption),
a baby giraffe, knees neat and folded, gazing long-lashed at
the adoring camera.

So many cute animals embedded in my folders.
No images of morose moray eels or disenchanted frogs
I might like to look at, might willingly embed, enfold.

Now please, friends, colleagues, neighbours, family,
I'm begging you, please, stop swamping me
with the cute and the cuddly.
It's all too much,
a kind of nature porn
I'm simply not into.

Apart from anything else – my memory is struggling.

The speed of summer

Hard red plum falls,
rolls down concrete apron –
fat fast blackbird waddles after.

The aviary

Inside me –
the bright-brown bantam
clucks her sonnet of contentment.
She dances the abundant garden,
replete in her shapely domesticity,
her compact completeness,
her questing eye.

Inside me –
the white-breasted sea eagle,
cool and controlled, patrols
headlands and solitary trees.
Lonely as an icon,
her full-stop eyes never miss
that crucial comma of fish
in the ocean's complex manuscript.

Inside me –
the angular heron
swoops into the garden pond,
pointing her teacher's beak
at indolent gold fish.
A meditation of steel-blue stillness,
elegant and precise,
she knows the tension of a meniscus,
monitors the slow revolutions
of orange flesh beneath green sunlight.

Inside me –
an aviary
alive with beaks and feathers,
soft cooing to soothe,
claws to slit open
your pale belly.

After, there are the birds

He sends me photos
of the singular crimson rosella
who observes him through the kitchen window
as he cooks dinner for one.

He sends me boxes of her best clothes:
designer jackets, silk shirts, tailored trousers.
Asks me to share them among family
even though she was the size of a wren
and we're all currawongs.

He sends me photo after poignant photo
of white-breasted sea eagles,
                    soaring   roosting   gliding.
Years before, knowing death might swoop,
she signed emails: 'from The White-Breasted Sea Eagle',
or sometimes, when energy was low: 'WBSE'.

He sends me photos of her grave
in a paddock so close to the ocean
sea eagles patrolling there
sense the running of rabbits and fish.

He sends me photos of the funeral,
me bearing her coffin with his three sisters,
my face bleak as a cliff
as we lay her in that space –
best birds-eye view of the ocean
and she –
without eyes.

He sends me news of the satin bowerbird
drowned in the liquid compost.
He retrieves the corpse, places it on an ants' nest.
Later, he sends the clean, exquisite skeleton
to an artist friend who draws skulls,
so frail, so strong.

There are no photos to send,
there can be no speaking of
how our sea eagle is composting now,   drowning
in the rich soil of her ocean paddock.
These, our desolate imaginings in that birdless hour,
round three in the morning…
        we simply cannot fly there together.

He sends me the last days' photos,
her three sisters and a niece bundled
beside the aluminium bed
we all knew so well   at the end.
We look so bonny and robin-round
beside her wren-bone frail.
She, still railing strong against
the determined flocks of starlings
roosting in her spine, liver, lungs.

He sends me copies of *Australian Birdlife,*
we speak of the plight of the orange-bellied parrot,
as the wind farms of loss
slice across his sky
as he attempts to migrate
from   *mated for life*
to   *flying solo.*

After my sister dies,
her husband says,   *Now,*
there is the company of birds.

Author photo: Ruiping

Gina Mercer enjoys a three-stranded career as a writer, teacher and editor. She's taught in universities and communities for nearly 30 years. She's a former editor of *Island*. She's published four collections of poetry: *The Ocean in the Kitchen* (1999); *Night Breathing* (2006); *Handfeeding the Crocodile* (2007); and *Seasoned with Honey* (with 3 other poets, 2008). She's published a novel, *Parachute Silk* (2001), plus two academic books. She's currently revelling in Tasmania.

Gina Mercer's poems are a delectable feast. Roll her words on your tongue. Savour their sound, the delicious and satisfying feel of them in your mouth.

Lyn Reeves

This is a lovely book to read. You know, a real joy. The work is delicate yet strong, sparse yet full. And love, how does it manage to infuse the whole without the word once being mentioned? This is powerful work yet somehow gentle at the same time. I love it.

Dr Robyn Rowland AO

Acknowledgements

I'd like to sincerely thank each of the editors of the publications: *Prospect*, *Blue Giraffe*, and *In Their Branches: Stories from ABC RN's Trees Project.* Thank you: Lyn Reeves, Pete Hay, Peter Macrow, and Gretchen Miller for publishing some of these poems.

My special thanks fly out to five poets who generously gave of their time and expertise and so helped this book out of the nest: Adrienne Eberhard, Pete Hay, Lyn Reeves, Robyn Rowland, and Deb Westbury.

I give a nest full of speckled eggs to each of my lovely friends whose conversation and companionship have nourished me: Tim Bass, Anne Collins, the FFIG, Shelly Hayes, the Pleiades, Mary Jenkins, Stephanie Lymburner, Liz McQuilkin, Lynn Romeo, Megan Schaffner, Maria Simms and Terry Whitebeach.

And a tree full of gang-gangs to my daughter, Lucy Mercer-Mapstone, and my partner, Bruce Mapstone. Your love and unwavering support keep me aloft.

Printed in Australia
AUOC02n0815220216
273934AU00011B/12/P